W9-ANX-469

THE
MAYA
INDIANS

THE JUNIOR LIBRARY OF
AMERICAN INDIANS

THE
MAYA
INDIANS

Victoria Sherrow

CHELSEA HOUSE PUBLISHERS
New York Philadelphia

FRONTISPIECE: Mayan carving of a noblewoman.

CHAPTER TITLE ORNAMENT: Artist's detail of a Mayan carving of Yax Pac, last king of the Classic Mayan site of Copán.

Chelsea House Publishers
EDITORIAL DIRECTOR Richard Rennert
EXECUTIVE MANAGING EDITOR Karyn Gullen Browne
EXECUTIVE EDITOR Sean Dolan
COPY CHIEF Robin James
PICTURE EDITOR Adrian G. Allen
ART DIRECTOR Robert Mitchell
MANUFACTURING DIRECTOR Gerald Levine
SYSTEMS MANAGER Lindsey Ottman
PRODUCTION COORDINATOR Marie Claire Cebrián-Ume

The Junior Library of American Indians
SENIOR EDITOR Sean Dolan

Staff for THE MAYA INDIANS
COPY EDITOR Nicole Greenblatt
EDITORIAL ASSISTANT Joy Sanchez
ASSISTANT DESIGNER John Infantino
PICTURE RESEARCHER Lisa Kirchner
COVER ILLUSTRATOR Shelly Pritchett

First Printing

1 3 5 7 9 8 6 4 2

Library of Congress Cataloging-in-Publication Data

Sherrow, Victoria.
The Maya Indians/Victoria Sherrow.
   p. cm.—(The Junior library of American Indians)
Summary: Discusses the history and culture of the Maya Indians, their daily routine, and the lives of their descendants.
      ISBN 0-7910-1666-8
      ISBN 0-7910-1994-2 (pbk.)
1. Mayas—Juvenile literature. [1. Mayas. 2. Indians of Central America.] I. Series.   93-21751
F1434.S547 1993   CIP
973.81'016—dc20   AC

CONTENTS

A carving of the ruler Yax Pac, Copán's last recorded king, in a temple at the Classic Mayan site of Copán.

CHAPTER **1**

Partners with the Gods

The ancient Maya believed that before the world began, there were only the sea and the empty sky. There were no trees, plants, stones, animals, birds, fish, or people. All was quiet. Hidden beneath feathers of green and blue, the two Creators looked out from the water. The Heart of Heaven cried out, "Let the earth appear! Let the light come!"

The creation began. Mountains sprang up through the water. Cypress trees and other plants spread their roots into the ground. The Creators looked upon the new land and the growing things. They decided that something was missing: human beings. People were needed so that the new world could reach its fullest glory. So the Creators set to work, making the first humans from the soil of the earth. But these humans had no minds. The Creators destroyed them. The Creators asked Grandmother Dawn for advice. "Read the corn," they begged her. "Read it to find out if we should make human beings of wood."

After casting the corn, Grandmother Dawn told them, "It is well that figures be made of wood."

The Creators did as she said, but the people made of wood had dry faces and no blood or hearts. They did not praise their makers. So they were also destroyed. Heavy, dark rains fell from the sky, and a flood carried the wooden ones away. The Creators tried again, saying, "Let human beings appear who will praise us." Then yellow and white ears of maize—corn—rose up from the seas. The Creators used the sacred grains of this maize to make the flesh of the new humans. These beings had perfect knowledge, but the Creators believed that too much knowledge was not a good thing. They asked the Heart of Heaven to chip at the peoples' eyes, so they would not see too much.

These were the first Mayan people, according to a sacred Mayan book called the *Popul Vuh*. Ancient Mayan priests told this creation

REGIONS WITHIN THE MAYA HOMELAND

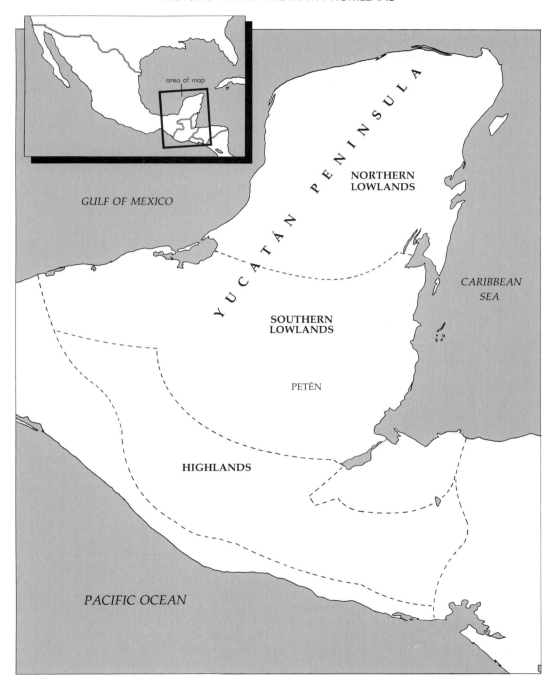

area of map

GULF OF MEXICO

YUCATÁN PENINSULA

NORTHERN
LOWLANDS

CARIBBEAN
SEA

SOUTHERN
LOWLANDS

PETÉN

HIGHLANDS

PACIFIC OCEAN

legend and other stories of Mayan history, stretching back some 4,000 years. In time, the tales were recorded, first with *hieroglyphics* (picture symbols), then in a written form using words.

The *Popul Vuh* set forth the beliefs and way of life of the Maya. They were expected to live as partners with the gods. Mayans believed that if they praised the gods and lived as the gods commanded, the gods would meet their earthly needs. The Mayan way of life meant fulfilling one's family and community duties. A good Mayan also had to take part in religious ceremonies and give sacrifices to the gods.

To guide the people, special priests studied the stars and other heavenly bodies and tried to understand people's dreams. The Mayans met with their religious leaders to discuss problems and make decisions about their lives.

The land was also important to the Maya. They occupied about 125,000 square miles in the Yucatán peninsula in southern Mexico, and part of Central America, including present-day Guatemala. The region is called *Mesoamerica* (meaning *middle* or *central* America).

The weather was different in the northern and southern parts of the Mayan's land. It was

A stone sculpture of the Mayan Maize God, found in a Copán palace. Corn was the most important crop for the Maya.

hot in the south, and there was a rain forest. In the north, the weather was drier but even hotter. Wherever they lived, the Mayans worked with the soil and weather to raise their crops. Often, they found clever ways to develop farm plots on wet areas or to get water to dry places.

The Maya learned to use the materials, plants, and animals that they found around them. They used these things to survive and to make their lives more pleasant. Their lands held volcanoes that gave the Maya valuable rock they could make into sharp tools. Fertile soil and a good climate for growing crops were great assets to the growth of Mayan society.

Corn was highly valued. It was the main crop of the Maya for thousands of years. The importance of corn can be seen even in the creation story, which tells of corn being used to make the flesh of humans. By improving the kind of corn they raised and adding new crops, the Maya could feed larger numbers of people. This helped them to increase their numbers and their influence in the region.

At the height of its power, the Mayan empire included a highly developed cultural life and vast trade network. Mayan city-states were rich and powerful. Thousands of public buildings and religious temples dotted the

Mayan lands of Central America. Yet, as the years passed, the Mayans lost their power. They were conquered by the Spanish who came to Mexico and Central and South America in the 1500s.

The Maya had to struggle to keep their valued customs and religion after the Spanish rulers came into power. Mayan descendants have faced many changes and problems since the 1500s and still do today, especially in Guatemala. In some other places, education, health, and economic conditions are slowly improving.

The Mayan culture is an important and fascinating part of human history. Historians have learned a great deal about Mayan knowledge, arts, and ancient way of life. Mayan architecture and belongings, including art treasures, have been found and studied. Excavations (dug-up areas) and the things found in them have helped 20th-century people to understand Mayan civilization and the way it influenced the growth of the Americas. ▲

A jade carving from the Olmec culture of a were-jaguar—a figure that is half-human and half-jaguar.

CHAPTER **2**

Ancient Roots

Thousands of years ago, the people who would later become known as the Maya lived in small groups scattered across Mexico and Central America. These bands of people survived by making simple but effective weapons and using them to hunt huge wild animals. Scientists who study ancient cultures have found caves where these people made their homes. By digging deep inside these caves, the scientists have uncovered objects used by the earliest Mayans. Among these items are pointed tips for arrows that date back 10,000 to 12,000 years.

In those days, herds of giant bison, woolly mammoth, and mastodon roamed in North and Central America. They fed on the lush

15

grasslands that were plentiful on these continents. But the weather in the Americas changed greatly at the end of a time period called the Ice Age. Enormous sheets of ice moved northward, and Central America became hotter and drier. The large herds of animals became extinct; that is, they died out.

After that, the bands of hunters had to look for smaller animals, such as deer and rabbits. An even more important source of food came from gathering wild plants. By about 7,000 B.C., these Native Americans began to settle in larger groups, forming villages. By growing their own corn, beans, and other crops, they were able to feed more people. For the next 5,000 years, they worked to grow better kinds of corn and other grains and vegetables. They changed from hunter-gatherers to farmers.

These people gradually moved into the Mesoamerican region that would hold the centers of Mayan civilization. One of these centers was located on the Yucatán Peninsula of southern Mexico. This peninsula (a piece of land that juts out into a lake or ocean) is almost surrounded by water: the Caribbean Sea is on the east and the Gulf of Campeche (the southwest end of the Gulf of Mexico) is on the west.

The Yucatán Peninsula is composed mostly of limestone, a type of rock made up of seashells and corals that have piled up over the centuries. The ancient Maya made good use of this limestone; they built many of their houses and temples from it. To work with the limestone, the Maya used tools made out of even harder stone. They also made tools from flint (an extremely hard mineral also called quartz), which they found embedded in the limestone. They chipped at the pieces of flint and made cutting and scraping tools from it.

The northern Yucatán is low and flat, with few lakes or other surface water. The rainy season lasts from May until October. During the rest of the year, this area is hot and dry. People living in the northern Yucatán had to find ways of getting water for drinking and growing crops. The animals in this land have also adapted to the dryness. Early Mayans called the Yucatán "the land of the turkey and the deer."

Below the northern tip of the Yucatán Peninsula are the lowlands. The earliest Mayan culture (known as the *Classic period*) developed in the lowland area between the third and ninth centuries A.D. The people found a wide variety of wildlife in this region's rain forest: boa constrictors, coral snakes, deadly pit vipers, howling monkeys, spider monkeys, scorpions, stinging insects, and spiders. For food, the ancient Maya hunted rabbits, deer, and turkeys. They also raised stingless bees for their honey, as Mayans still do today.

Another region settled by the ancient Maya lies next to the Pacific Ocean and includes present-day Guatemala. In the forest of this area lives the rare *quetzal*, a bird with brilliant green feathers that has become the symbol of Guatemala. The region is sometimes disturbed by earthquakes and volcanic eruptions, but it has fertile volcanic soil and a springlike climate. These conditions have attracted many settlers to this region during the past 3,000 years.

In 1960, scientist Richard MacNeish and his assistants were studying Mexican caves where ancient Mayans had lived when they made an exciting discovery. While digging deep in a cave in Mexico's Tehuacán Valley, they found signs that people had lived there over a period of about 12,000 years. MacNeish later wrote, "Working downward, we found that the cave had 28 separate occupation levels, the earliest of which may date to about 10,000 B.C." MacNeish was also delighted when the group found "six corncobs, three of which looked more primitive and older than any I had seen before." Later,

One of many giant stone faces found at the Olmec site of San Lorenzo. Historians believe that the heads may represent royal Olmecs.

laboratory studies showed that this corn was about 5,600 years old.

By about 1500 B.C., a group now called the *Olmec* had created a successful way of life that would influence the later Mayans. The Olmecs lived in a hot region in what is now Veracruz, Mexico. The Olmecs were skillful farmers, and their land contained areas of rich soil as well as rivers. Their villages were led by powerful chiefs. They traded with other Native Americans, carved ornate stone monuments, and worshipped many gods. They developed calendars to measure time.

An old Olmec center now called San Lorenzo shows the complex features of their way of life. The people of San Lorenzo were divided into classes of nobles and commoners, all ruled by one chief. The chief was in charge of political and religious matters. Between 1200 and 900 B.C., the nobles of San Lorenzo planned projects that required

laborers to build ornate monuments, including one topped by many giant stone heads.

Historians think these stone faces portray royal Olmecs. The workers carried untold numbers of baskets of silt, used to make finger-shaped ridges for the monument. Back and forth they must have trudged, toting millions of cubic feet of earth for this project.

Something strange took place in about 700 B.C. to end life in San Lorenzo. *Archaeologists*—scientists who study people and cultures from earlier periods in history—have tried to figure out what happened at that time. They have dug up stone carvings of animals and humans that were beheaded and smashed on purpose, as if to "kill" them, then buried. The religious altars of San Lorenzo were also ruined at that time. Did enemies invade the city and cause this destruction? Or did the people themselves destroy their monuments and carvings and then choose to die, for some reason? The answer remains a mystery.

Other Olmec people lived around the center called La Venta for about 500 years after San Lorenzo's demise. These people also had fine carvings and fancy monuments. A

This small carving represents an Olmec god. It was worn around the neck by a king, showing that he had a connection with the supernatural.

class system of nobles and commoners existed at La Venta as it had in San Lorenzo. Olmec artists used jade to make especially fine objects, which include carvings of the were-jaguar, a figure that is part jaguar, part human. Some later Mayan artwork contains figures that link Mayan history to that of the Olmec. By 100 B.C., the Olmecs' civilization had ended. Perhaps the growth of other trade centers in Mesoamerica took away their power in the region. They also may have stopped gathering the wealth that they received when they controlled trade in the region.

Historians have found two other powerful trade centers that were becoming more important at this time. One was Teotihuacán in the valley of Mexico. The second was Kaminaljuyú, located in the highlands of present-day Guatemala. From about 1,000 B.C. to A.D. 600, Kaminaljuyú served as a strong link in the north-south trade routes. Raw jade and obsidian were among the most profitable trade items for the rulers and other members of Kaminaljuyú society.

The lavish tombs designed for the Kaminaljuyú chiefs show that this place held great wealth. Archaeologists have found these tombs under huge earthen mounds that consist of several pyramids. The pyramids, built one above the other, were made of adobe that workers mixed from water, soil, clay, and grass, adding bits of pottery for strength.

Inside one such pyramid, diggers uncovered a rectangular-shaped tomb holding a man's body. It had been painted bright red and was dressed in rich clothing for the burial. The body was surrounded with furnishings the person might have needed in the afterlife, along with jade ornaments, gifts, and offerings for the gods. Three other bodies were found buried with this nobleman. They may have been killed as sacrifices in order to accompany their master into the afterlife as servants.

The settlement at Kaminaljuyú began to weaken about A.D. 200. It seems that traders and warriors from the other main trade center, Teotihuacán, moved in, either as invaders or by invitation. A new culture developed that used parts of both the older ones. This can be seen in certain tombs; built in the old way of Kaminaljuyú, they contain items made with the artistic styles of Teotihuacán.

For about 700 years, Teotihuacán was the most important city in Central America. At its peak, it had about 200,000 residents, and it controlled the region's trade and political and religious life. It also contained two remark-

A ceremonial container found at Kaminaljuyú.

able buildings. One, the Pyramid of the Sun, was built in A.D. 125 and stood as high as a modern 20-story building. At its top was a religious temple, decorated with huge ornaments, bright flowers, and dazzling green quetzal feathers. The Pyramid of the Moon was likewise a grand building.

Around A.D. 700, Teotihuacán too declined. The problems leading to its end may have come from disputes among leaders or from a failure of local crops. In any case, people abandoned the city. But hundreds of years later, the Aztec Indians of Mexico began to visit the ruins, calling it "the place of the gods." These centers and ways of life became the heart of the golden age of the Classic Mayan culture that would follow.

This culture was a farming economy based on maize, which the people raised along with beans, squash, and manioc (cassava). The Maya also grew cotton, which they spun, dyed, and wove into cloth with great skill. Although these early Mayans had no wheels or beasts of burden, they did have domesticated dogs and turkeys. By about A.D. 250, villages of people and their cornfields were spread throughout Mesoamerica. The prosperous age of the Classic Maya was about to begin. ▲

CHAPTER **3**

Life Among the Maya

The Classic Maya period was a time of powerful rulers, grand buildings, and other achievements in art, mathematics, and science. This culture flowered from the third to the ninth centuries. Fortunately, the Maya recorded important historical events, first with pictures, then with written symbols. Their records have enabled modern historians to describe what life was like during this time.

Early Mayan scribes noted important events and their dates using hieroglyphics. These pictures can be seen on Mayan monuments, walls, and other places. When the hieroglyphs were first found, historians did not recognize their meaning. But in 1958, some historians realized that the pictures followed certain patterns and might describe Mayan rulers, places, and events. By figuring out what the pictures meant, historians have learned much about the Classic period.

Certain centers of Mayan life played an especially important role in the development of the Classic period. One such city, Tikal, was built in the rain forest of northern Guatemala. Tikal was founded about 3,000 years ago when people settled among the huge ceiba trees, which the Maya considered sacred. The art found in Tikal shows that this jungle was then, as it is now, home to hundreds of different birds, including colorful parrots, golden turkeys, and hummingbirds. Spider monkeys and snakes also lived in the jungle, along with jaguars, pumas, deer, and ocelots, all of which now roam near the ruins of the city of Tikal.

Tikal's people may have settled there because the area is so rich in flint. The Maya could make this hard but fine-textured mineral into tools and weapons or trade it for other goods. Trade must have been important for this city. Old tombs found there contain seashells from the coast, as well as jade and pottery that must have come from the highlands of Guatemala.

Water was a problem because no rivers run across this land. The people of Tikal relied upon water holes called *aguadas*. By build-

The back and front of a jade pendant called the Leyden Plate. It shows a Mayan king, most likely Jaguar Paw.

ing walls of land around reservoirs (water storage areas), they provided themselves with water for drinking and farming during the dry seasons.

The ruins at Tikal show that the people built large and impressive temples, shrines, and tombs, as well as other buildings. By studying these ruins, archaeologists guess that people worked on these buildings over a period of more than 1,000 years. While the nobles lived in fine palaces, the commoners made their homes in small, thatch-roofed huts.

Strong, ambitious kings worked to make Tikal powerful. The first ruler may have been Jaguar Paw, whose rule began about A.D. 320. A jade pendant called the Leyden Plate shows a king who is thought to be Jaguar Paw. The king's clothing and ornaments contain signs that the gods meant for him to rule. They show that he was a great warrior. Jaguar Paw also wears a special headdress decorated with god heads, the main one being a jaguar.

The next ruler was probably a man now known as Curl Nose. Under his leadership, Tikal gained great power and became wealthier. His son, whom modern historians have named Stormy Sky, took over after his father's death in 426 and ruled until 457. Stormy Sky became the most important of

Tikal's Early Classic rulers. He got control of new trade routes and brought fine goods to his kingdom. Tikal became the most powerful place in the central lowlands. It also seems that Tikal became more closely tied to Teotihuacán during this time.

Carvings show Stormy Sky surrounded by guards wearing Teotihuacán military helmets and carrying shields with pictures of one of their gods, Tlaloc, the Lightning-Hurler Rain God. Pictures of Stormy Sky show a richly dressed, bejeweled ruler. He wears a royal belt that has a jaguar head both in front and in back. His headdress is laden with fancy carved jade ornaments.

It is unclear who became the ruler of Tikal after Stormy Sky died. It may have been his son, Kan Boar. After that, from 488 to 537, Jaguar Paw Skull, the heir of Kan Boar, was king. Tikal began to lose its political power and its economic control in the southern region. At about the same time, Teotihuacán also lost its influence.

In about 682, a new ruler named Ah Cacau helped Tikal regain its power. New buildings were put up, and the number of people in the city grew to about 45,000. To celebrate his success, Ah Cacau ordered a massive new temple, the Temple of the Giant Jaguar, to be built in the city. Inside the temple is a carving of a woman's head, perhaps Ah Cacau's wife.

King Ah Cacau ordered the Temple of the Giant Jaguar to be built in Tikal. The temple contains the king's tomb.

The Temple of the Giant Jaguar contains the king's tomb, which held his body along with many ornaments made of jade, pearls, seashells, and other precious materials.

Like other Mayan centers, Tikal went through cycles of growth, prosperity, and decline over a period of centuries. By the end of the 900s, the city was being neglected. From then on, the rain forest would grow over and around the ruins until they were dug up in the late 1800s.

Other centers were important during the Classic Maya period. One was Yaxchilan, also located in the rain forest. This place was ruled by a line of kings that historians call the Jaguar dynasty. Panels on the temple of this city tell the history of Yaxchilan's rulers. They show scenes in which enemies are captured and neighboring kingdoms are defeated as this center rose to power. Other pictures show religious ceremonies and sacrifices.

Around A.D. 600, Tikal and Yaxchilan were among four main centers of Classic Maya life. In the southwestern region, Palenque was the main center. Copán was the ruling center of the southeast. Rulers enjoyed a life of wealth and privilege, living in fine palaces with many servants. Some kings were fierce warriors who showed their courage by taking part in hand-to-hand fighting. Rulers and other nobles wore fine clothing with decorative headdresses and jewelry.

The Maya hunted jaguars, the world's largest spotted cats. These animals' magnificent pelts (coats) were made into cloaks for nobles and military leaders. Surrounded by fine buildings and lavish works of art, the Mayan rulers continued to expand their power and bring more wealth to their kingdoms. The city of Palenque, in the Chiapas highlands, was a good example of the splendor of the Classic period.

Palenque was built on hills that faced a lush forest-covered plain. Fruit trees grew wild, and plenty of fish swam in the waters. Beautiful flowers bloomed all around the city, adorning the red-painted temples and

A Mayan head sculpture found in Pacal's tomb in Palenque. Pacal ruled the city from A.D. 615–683.

pyramids. A king known as Pacal ruled the city from A.D. 615 to 683. When he died, his subjects built a magnificent temple to hold his tomb and to honor him. The stone that was carved to hold Pacal's body weighed some 25 tons (50,000 pounds). Many laborers must have spent long hours hollowing it out. Over the tomb, workers built a pyramid-temple.

When the tomb was opened and studied in 1952, amazing objects were found inside of it. Within a room of shining walls, Pacal's coffin stood surrounded by sculptures of tall guards. The lid of the coffin was covered with elaborate carved pictures of the king, a ceiba tree, heavenly bodies, the three afterworlds, gods, and other symbols. The body of Pacal was wrapped in red cotton and lay amid piles of jade and pearl jewelry. His face was covered with a jade mosaic mask.

Prosperity helped the Maya to develop their arts and other types of knowledge. One remarkable achievement was in the use of mathematics. The Mayan number system used just three symbols. A bar meant the number five, a dot stood for one, and a shell was used for zero. The idea of having a symbol for zero, or nothing, is especially notable. In those days, most other civilizations had not yet come up with the idea of a symbol that could stand for the concept

										positional values	
									●●●●	x 144 000	baktun
									▬▬	x 7200	katun
							●●●	⬯	⬯	x 360	tun
						●	▬	⬯	●●●●	x 20	uinal
⬯	●	●●●●	▬	▬▬	●●●●	⬯	▬	▬▬	●●	⬯	x 1	kin
0	1	4	5	11	19	20	126	1092	36 102	1 368 080 days	

The Mayan numerical system—a bar meant the number five, a dot stood for one, and a shell symbolized zero.

of nothing. By combining these three symbols—a bar, a dot, a shell—the Maya could show numbers from 0 to 19. Numbers higher than 19 were shown by the position of the symbols.

Skillful use of mathematics improved other parts of Mayan life. The priests used numbers to develop and read different kinds of calendars. Three types of calendars had come down to the Classic Maya from earlier civilizations. Priests used different calendars to mark important events in the lives of the rulers, to plan farming activities and ceremonies, and to record the movements of the planets and stars.

Of course, most of the Mayan people were not rulers, nobles, astronomers, or priests. The common people, including workers, craftsmen, farmers, toolmakers, and weavers, were the backbone of the society.

It was their skill and energy that made day-to-day life possible.

Having enough food let the Maya keep stable cities and towns and enrich other areas of life. Maize was the Mayans' chief food, as it was for many Native American groups in the region. The Mayas in both the highlands and lowlands have raised corn for about 4,000 years.

During the Classic period, Mayan farmers planted and raised corn by methods that some farmers use today. When starting new cornfields, called *milpas*, they chose well-drained forest areas when possible. To clear the land for planting, the Mayan farmer cut down trees and burned any low-growing brush. Ancient Maya used stone tools to cut away vines and young trees growing on the land. The farmer usually did such clearing in late autumn. When the dead trees and brush had dried, he set fire to them.

At planting time, the Mayan farmer moved across the field with a sack of maize kernels over his shoulder. His main tool was a digging stick with one end hardened by fire. He poked a hole in the soil, then dropped in a few corn kernels and often a bean seed, too. The bean plant's long vines would curl around the corn plant as it grew. From May to September, the farmer kept busy weeding his fields. When the ears of corn began to ripen, he bent the stalks down so that rain could not get inside and allow mold to grow. Late fall was harvest time.

When the soil in a field tired after many plantings, the farmer started another. The Mayans found ways to make new milpas from swamps. They piled up soil between ditches to make fresh plots. They also made fields on hills, building stone walls to keep the soil from wearing away. Along with the larger fields, they grew crops in small gardens near their houses.

Corn made up about 80 percent of the ancient Mayan diet. In both ancient and modern times, Mayan women have used corn to make nourishing meals. Corn cakes are usually made fresh each day. To soften the dry kernels, the cook mixes them with water and lime. She brings the combination to a boil, then lets it sit until the next day. After washing the corn, she throws out the hulls.

Classic Mayans ground corn with a *mano*— a hand-held stone—onto a flat stone called a *metate*. Modern cooks use more up-to-date kitchen tools. In both cases, this patient work produces a thick dough. The cook forms a lump of the dough the size of a hen's egg and pats it over and over to make thin, flat corn cakes called tortillas.

Tortillas are baked on a heated stone griddle over a fire. By midday, the delicious-smelling corn cakes are ready. Hungry children can hope to find one staying hot inside a gourd. Sometimes, the cakes are topped with honey. Or they may be stuffed with meat: turkey, deer, or duck.

The Mayan way of life called for a vast number of laborers. Workers were responsible for providing the food and fuel that other citizens needed each day. A great many Mayans worked on the large building projects. Some workers cut out and carried the stones, and some planned and put up the temples and other buildings. It took many strong men to carry such heavy loads without the help of pack animals.

The making of fine cloth was an important industry. Some people grew and harvested the cotton crop. Expert spinners and weavers made both simple designs for commoners and fancy dyed clothing for the nobles. Along with these craftsmen, there were toolmakers and people who made products such as pottery, walls, thatched roofing, and canoes.

Spiritual customs were important to the Classic Maya, and religion guided them in daily life. They believed in three supernatural worlds: the Upperworld, Middleworld, and Underworld. The sacred ceiba tree stood at the center of the universe and joined the three worlds. The tree's branches reached toward the Upperworld. Its trunk was in line with the Middleworld, and the roots spread downward toward the Underworld. The Mayans believed that after death souls moved from the lower to the higher worlds by means of the ceiba tree.

The Upperworld's main feature was the sun passing across the sky. Priests studied the sun, moon, and planets because they were thought to affect life for good or bad. The Middleworld was marked by special birds, trees, and colors.

A number of gods were important to the Maya. Itzamna, the chief god, is pictured as a two-headed sky serpent. His wife, Ix Chel, was the goddess of weaving, medicine, and childbirth. The Mayans believed that all other gods were born from this couple. Another important idol, the Sun God, had a fascinating double nature. Its day nature was the bright sun that moved across the heavens each day. At night, the Sun God kept moving, but through the dark Underworld, or "place of fright." There, the sun became the fearful Jaguar God. Also in the Underworld were gods of death. One of them, Yum Cimil, is pictured as monstrous-looking, with a bony face and swollen body.

The Rain Gods and the Maize God were respected for their role in promoting good

A sketch of Lady Kan-Ik, Pacal's grandmother, based on a carving in the king's tomb.

crops. As part of their religious customs, the Maya gave blood sacrifices to their gods. People gave blood to show respect to the gods during important events, such as burials, temple dedications, crop plantings, and child namings. The giving of blood symbolized the people's connection to the supernatural world. They might pierce their tongues and let blood fall onto a paper. The paper was then burned, so that the smoke would rise up to the gods. Prisoners who were taken in battle were killed in formal ceremonies according to Mayan customs.

By the 900s, the Classic period had survived for several centuries. Generations of Mayans were born, got married, raised children, and followed their ancient customs. But after 799, the different centers began to decline. By about 909, Palenque, Tikal, Toniná, and Bonampak were no longer rich, powerful cities with many people. No longer did their citizens erect large, fancy buildings. Perhaps these centers suffered from bad leadership, wars, hunger, or plagues of some kind. Today, no one knows exactly what happened. At any rate, another stage of Mayan history, with its own strengths and accomplishments, was soon to begin. ▲

A mural from Chichén Itzá showing the activities of everyday life in a Mayan village.

CHAPTER 4

A Changing Empire

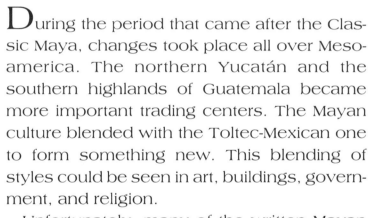

During the period that came after the Classic Maya, changes took place all over Mesoamerica. The northern Yucatán and the southern highlands of Guatemala became more important trading centers. The Mayan culture blended with the Toltec-Mexican one to form something new. This blending of styles could be seen in art, buildings, government, and religion.

Unfortunately, many of the written Mayan histories from the Post-classic period no longer exist. They were lost during the Spanish conquest of the 1500s. The few native manuscripts that survived are being carefully studied by modern historians. One such book is called the *Dresden Codex*, and is thought to be a 12th-century copy of an older book. Mayan priests used this book to chart the movements of heavenly bodies and to record ceremonies, rules, and predictions for the future.

The Mayan histories also tell stories of traders and foreigners who came to Mayan lands by sea. A group called Putun Maya were powerful merchants and warriors. They gained control of the profitable salt trade. Cacao, honey, and other food items, as well as various goods—cotton cloth, seashells, raw jade, obsidian, and feathers—were traded. The Maya also sold people as slaves, moving them from place to place.

To conquer more land, the powerful Putun probably joined with important *Toltec* warriors from Mexico. They then developed a capital at Chichén Itzá. With the passing years, the Putun took on more traits and practices of the Toltec-Mexican culture. As they traveled south, they brought these Mexican ways of life with them.

The Toltec influenced the Maya to add one of their gods, Quetzalcoatl, to their religious practices. The symbol of Quetzalcoatl—a feathered snake with wide-open jaws—appears on many Mayan buildings in the Yucatán. Large numbers of warriors, jaguars, and snakes appear on Mayan objects made during this time. At the center of Chichén Itzá stood a massive building, the Temple of the

continued on page 49

CLAY FIGURINES

A Jaina figurine of a dwarf dressed as a warrior. Strung through his earlobes are paper strips that were worn by participants in blood-letting rituals.

Jaina is a small island off the coast of the Yucatán Peninsula. During the Mayan's late Classic period (A.D. 700–900), large tombs were built on this island, filled with ornaments and decorative objects for the dead to use in the afterlife.

Hundreds of clay figurines of 5 to 10 inches were found in the Jaina tombs. The figures were crafted by hand or by using molds, then painted blue, yellow, red, green, and white. Some figures have whistles in their backs, and others are filled with pebbles so they make noise when they are shaken.

Most of the Jaina figurines are of Mayan nobles, dressed in different costumes. However, there are also figures of people who were not normally represented in other Mayan works, such as court entertainers. The facial features of the figurines were extremely realistic, more so than those of most Mayan sculpture. The Jaina figurines were possibly small portraits of actual people and thus were the most expressive of all Mayan artwork.

This figurine represents a captive of war. His contorted body and howls of pain are evidence that he has been tortured by his captors.

A warrior wearing a costume and helmet made of feathers. In some Maya paintings, warriors dressed like jaguars are shown defeating fighters in this type of clothing.

Like many other Jaina warrior figurines, this figure's face is marked with swirls that suggest elaborate face paint.

A seated noble wearing ball-playing regalia, including a jaguar-claw necklace and a protective garment made from a jaguar hide.

Dressed in a traditional huipil and elaborate jewelry, this regal woman weaving on a loom probably represents the moon goddess.

In this figurine, a moon goddess embraces an aging god. Sculptures such as this were probably buried in the tombs of elderly men.

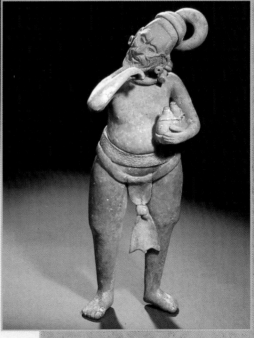

Through this figure's highly expressive features and posture, its maker communicated the bewilderment of a drunk old man.

45

Wearing armor, this seated lord is dressed for war. The detachable headdress beside the figurine is constructed from an arc of feathers above a monstrous mask of an animal skull with a large gaping mouth.

Right: With the headdress hiding the lord's human face, he becomes a terrifying figure.

A ruler seated on an intricately carved throne covered by a jaguar pelt. He wears earflares, a wide collar, and a three-paneled cape.

The lid of the sarcophagus of Pacal, who ruled the city of Palenque between 615 and 683. The carving on the lid shows the moment of Pacal's death. From below, the Maw of the Underworld is rising up to engulf the ruler. Above Pacal is the World Tree at the center of the universe. The image, thus, depicts Pacal's descent from Earth to the Underworld.

continued from page 40

Warriors. Towering serpent columns stood at the entrance of this immense structure, which may have been the headquarters of the government. Carved on the rows of columns were weapon-carrying Toltec officers and women bringing offerings to the gods.

The Toltec-Maya warriors, including Jaguar knights and Eagle knights, were in charge of capturing prisoners who would be killed for religious sacrifices. Priests offered the human hearts from such victims to the sun. These offerings may have been placed in sculpted human figures called *chacmools*. The hands of these stone figures held bowl-shaped containers for offerings.

The Toltec-Maya were devoted to various types of ball games, some of which had a religious meaning. They built special courts on which to play. The Great Ball Court, located across from the Temple of the Warriors, is the largest of its kind in Mesoamerica. About 400 ball courts have been found in places where the Maya lived. The games seem to date back at least 4,000 years.

There are no writings that tell the rules of these games. Europeans who came to Mesoamerica in the 1500s described how they were played at that time. Players from two teams used a solid rubber ball, weighing about eight pounds. To score, they had to make this bouncing ball hit the opponents' side of the court or go through a ring hanging high alongside the court. The game was quite difficult because players could only use their elbows, wrists, or hips—never their hands—to strike the ball.

Players chasing low-bouncing balls risked getting hurt when they hit the stone or plaster floor. To protect themselves, they wore leather or cotton pads on their knees and elbows. This equipment was highly valued. Families passed it down to their children and grandchildren. Spectators enjoyed watching this exciting sport. They also gambled, sometimes with their jewelry and clothing, on who would win. When they saw the final point being made, those who had bet on the wrong team fled from the court. The successful bettors and players chased after them to collect their winnings.

Some carved scenes at the Chichén Itzá Ball Court suggest that the game may have been played for life and death, and that there may have been some religious ceremonies involved. Those who were defeated may have been beheaded with knives by the winning players. Other gruesome pictures show a head being used as a ball in the game. Above the ball are pictures of plants, signs of fertility.

The Maya thought that the gods needed human parts, especially hearts and blood, or they could not keep the earth fertile. Sacrifices were also made to the Rain Gods, called *Chacs*. The northern Yucatán is dry. People settled near sources of underground water so they could make wells.

The well at Chichén Itzá became a sacred shrine. To please the gods, the priests offered sacrifices of people and fine goods. In the 1500s, a Spanish bishop wrote, "Into this well they had . . . the custom of throwing men

The Temple of the Warriors, located at the center of the Toltec-Mayan city of Chichén Itzá.

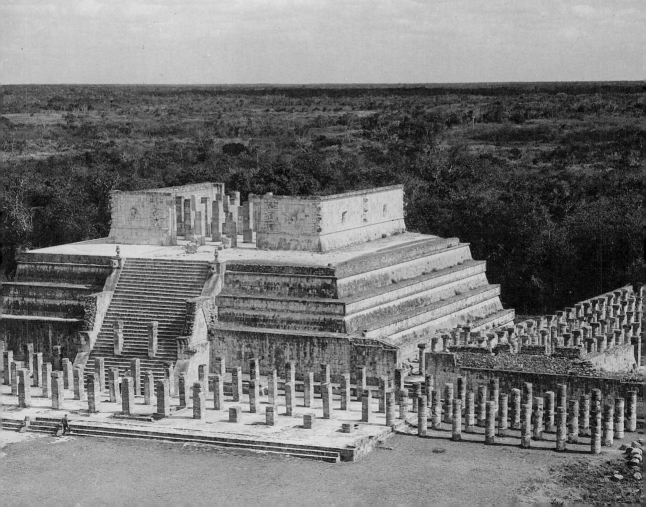

A chacmool in Chichén Itzá. The hands of the sculpted human figure held containers for offerings.

alive, as a sacrifice to the gods in times of drought (lack of rain), and they believed they did not die though they never saw them again. They also threw in many other things, like precious stones and things that they prized."

By this time, many goods came to the region from other lands. In the well, there were gold objects from Panama and Costa Rica, jade and obsidian from Guatemala, and copper from Mexico. Rubber from tree sap was shaped into balls, painted, then studded with jade and shells to make gifts for the gods. Wooden objects, copper bells, shells, and fancy pottery were also thrown into the well.

A turning point in Mayan history came in the late 1200s. The Toltec-Maya somehow lost their great power. At about this time, the important center of Tula fell. There was fighting among different groups of people who had moved to Chichén Itzá from other places. Later, Cocom, a man descended from Itzá royalty, managed to get control of Mayapan. Founded in 1263, Mayapan replaced Chichén Itzá as the Yucatán capital in about 1283.

Mayapan had been planned as a military city. There was a high wall around it. It had no temples or ball courts, but only a poorly built pyramid in the middle of the city. The chiefs of Mayapan increased their power by choosing marriage partners from ruling families. One of Cocom's descendants, Hunac Ceel, joined his kingdom with another called Izabal and gained more power and valuables for his people. His descendants were able to rule the Yucatán region until 1450.

During the 1440s, some Mexican nobles from a family called Xiu claimed the right to rule. They led a revolt in Mayapan, killing the Cocom king and all his sons except one who was in Honduras. The kingdom gradually fell apart. It broke up into different regional states, each led by chiefs who kept fighting among themselves.

For years, Mayapan suffered from many problems. Ah Dzun Xiu, grandson of the Xiu who had led the revolt in Mayapan, hoped he could make peace with the gods to end the troubles. He planned a religious journey to the sacred well in Chichén Itzá, called the

Cenote of Sacrifice. To get there, he would have to pass through land ruled by Nachi Cocom, great-grandson of the Cocom whom the Xiu family had killed years before.

Nachi Cocom told Xiu he could pass through his lands safely. Meanwhile, he was planning revenge. He invited Xiu and his fellow travelers to a great feast. When they arrived, the Cocoms killed them all. The murders increased old feelings of hatred among the people in the Yucatán. Civil wars and diseases further weakened the people living in the different states.

Mayan kingdoms in the southern highlands also declined during this Post-classic period. By the 1500s, there were a number of separate states, as in the north. Quiché Maya and Cakchiquel Maya were the strongest. They may have been settled by descendants of the Putun Maya who had come to the highlands in about 1200.

A leader called Feathered Serpent led groups of soldiers, based in strong mountain camps. They raided towns and took control of the region. In the 1400s, Feathered Serpent started a new capital, Utatlán. He was a fierce king who collected many goods in tribute (taxes) from those he ruled. He continued to start wars and overthrow other leaders until the Spanish arrived in Mesoamerica.

A Guatemalan Mayan man photographed in 1937, carrying his load with a strap around his forehead. This is the way the Maya carried heavy objects before the Spaniards introduced them to horses and donkeys.

The Spanish conquerors of the 1500s arrived to find the people of Mesoamerica no longer united. But the Mayans had developed a remarkable sea trade in 600 years. A major trade item was salt from the northern coastline of the Yucatán. Canoes from Itzá carried obsidian, copper, and fine cloth to trade for valuable salt and honey. Further south, in Honduras, these traders loaded their canoes with stone metates and axes.

The salt marshes in the Yucatán greatly impressed the Spanish newcomers. Taking over the salt trade and the other wealth of the area became a major goal of these Europeans. Though the Mayans were to lose their wealth and lands, they succeeded in maintaining valued parts of their culture. ⏶

A woodcut showing Spanish conquistadores abusing their Indian bearers.

CHAPTER 5

Intruders from Spain

Mayan priests had predicted that strangers would one day arrive to conquer their land. Yet the sight of the Spaniards, in a ship with towering sails, must have surprised the Mayans. In 1502, one of Christopher Columbus's ships came upon a Mayan canoe off the coast of Honduras. Columbus's teenage son later said the canoe had been carved from one large tree trunk. It was a trading canoe, holding copper axes, pottery, fine clothing, and other goods. The "bearded men," as the Maya would call the Spaniards, took the canoe and its cargo. During the struggle, cacao beans, used as money by the Maya, scattered on the floor. Columbus's son said that the Mayans rushed to get them "as if they were their eyes."

Pedro de Alvarado, a soldier under Hernán Cortés, led the Spanish conquest of the Maya in Guatemala in 1523. His ruthless invasions included burning villages and killing the inhabitants.

A 16th-century Spanish explorer, Bernardo Díaz del Castillo, said the Spanish invaders wanted two things: "To bring light to those in darkness, and also to get rich." For the next 300 years, the Spanish continued to come to Mesoamerica, as well as to Mexico and South America. They took the Mayans' land and forced the people to work for them. Spanish priests demanded that the Mayans give up their religion and follow Christian teachings.

Many Mayans tried to oppose the Spanish conquerors. But their enemies had larger numbers of soldiers and guns. They also brought deadly diseases, such as smallpox and measles, to Native Americans. The Indians had never had these diseases before. Their people did not have any natural body resistance or immunity to fight them off. Widespread diseases killed thousands of people and whole cities and armies.

By 1520, the Spanish soldiers under Hernán Cortés had defeated the Aztec Indians of Mexico. Cortés sent some of his soldiers, led by Pedro de Alvarado, to conquer the Maya in Guatemala. A Spanish historian wrote that Alvarado "advanced killing, ravaging, burning, robbing, and destroying all the country."

The Spanish treated the Mayans cruelly and unjustly, then expected them to agree to follow a king who lived in a land they had never seen. Alvarado's troops, led by a man called Tecum, the king's grandson, defeated the Quiché Maya. After Tecum was killed in battle, the Quiché asked Alvarado to visit their capital, Utatlán. But Alvarado did not trust the Mayans. He fled from the city just before the Mayans were able to kill him, as they had planned.

The Spanish then invaded Utatlán and captured the Mayan leaders. They burned the city, along with many of the leaders. The other powerful Guatemalan Mayans, the Cakchiquel, tried to join with the invading Spaniards. But the Spanish soon upset them, and the Indians rebelled. Alvarado insisted that the Mayans give him all their gold. If they refused, he said, "I shall burn you alive and hang you." By 1527, the Spanish controlled the highlands. The Mayans, who had once ruled in splendor, had become little more than slaves to the new rulers.

The conquest of the Yucatán was more difficult for the Spanish. Francisco Fernández de Córdoba, a Spanish explorer, had arrived there in 1517. The Spanish soldiers rode horseback and had fierce dogs. They carried guns, which the Mayans called thunder sticks. Even so, the Mayans fought so hard they rid their homeland of the invaders. Cordoba received 33 wounds and later died.

Hernán Cortés invaded Cozumel Island, off the Mexican coast, in 1519. Alvarado, del Castillo, and Francisco de Montejo helped him conquer the Aztec empire, and in 1527, the king of Spain ruled that the Yucatán should become a colony. Montejo and his son, Montejo the Younger, led a 20-year fight to defeat the Maya of the Yucatán. With their weapons—arrows, poles, swords, and sharp-tipped spears—the Mayans tried to keep the invaders out. But 1,200 of them died, and at last the Mayan chiefs surrendered.

Even so, there was so much Mayan protest against Spanish rule that the conquistadores had to return in 1531 for another battle, this one lasting four years. Montejo the Younger set up a royal capital at Chichén Itzá. He divided the towns and villages among his soldiers, with each man getting control of about 2,000 to 3,000 Mayans. The Xiu Mayans who lived in a province called Mani

A painting of a Mayan nobleman holding a ceremonial bar.

decided to welcome the Spaniards and become their allies.

Montejo was faced with problems when many of his soldiers left the Yucatán to go search for gold in Peru. And in 1541, Montejo the Younger left for the ancient ruins of Tiho, where he founded a new city, Mérida. Because the Xius were not fighting the Spaniards, some other western regions agreed not to resist them also. But the Cocom of Sotuta and some eastern provinces resisted the Spanish, leading to many bloody battles and numerous Mayan deaths.

In November 1546, the united Mayans fought their last battle. For four months, they defended their land fiercely. They caught some Spaniards and tortured them, but in the end they were defeated. The Mayans in the Yucatán had fought the conquerors longer than any other group in Mesoamerica. But now, the entire peninsula was under Spanish rule.

The Spanish killed about 500,000 Mayans, but many still remained. The Spanish controlled these people with strict laws. Mayans were forced into labor and into the Christian religion. Priests from the order of St. Francis were given some government duties. They ordered the Indians to be baptized, and put the sons of the Mayan nobles into church-run schools where they were taught obedience to the Spaniards and the Catholic church. The priests also moved the Indians to more central locations. In order to do so, they removed some Mayans from their homes, then burned their houses, along with their fruit trees and their few belongings.

The Mayans had looked upon the land and food as sacred gifts. They did not understand that to the Spanish, these "gifts" were seen as ways to get wealthy. They suffered greatly from the way the Spanish treated them. One

The Church of St. Francis in Guadalajara, Mexico. Priests from the Franciscan order in Spain were given the duty of converting the Maya to Christianity.

ruler, Diego de Landa, criticized the way his fellow Spaniards treated the Maya. Yet he himself severely beat or hanged Mayans who were caught practicing their ancient religion. In three months, Landa had more than 4,500 Indians tortured. He burned 27 Mayan hieroglyphic religious books, saying they held "the lies of the devil." But Landa has also been praised for writing a detailed history book of Mayan culture.

As time passed, new ways of life took shape. With the consent of Spanish rulers in the cities, Mayan nobles were allowed to govern the rural areas. A religion that blended Roman Catholic beliefs and Christian saints with Mayan gods unfolded. In the eastern and southern areas, many Mayans went back to their old religion.

The Spanish and Mayan cultures continued to mix. People from the two groups married through the years, resulting in *mestizos*—people of mixed Indian and Spanish descent. New farm crops, such as sugarcane, were raised for profitable trade. A plant called henequen was raised for its fibers, which are made into rope. As Spaniards set up large plantations called *haciendas*, the Indians lost more of their land and ways to make a living. This and other changes made during the 19th and 20th centuries had a great impact on how the Maya live today. ⚊

A photograph taken in the late 1800s of the henequen harvest in the Yucatán. The crop, called green gold, was used in making twine and made the Yucatán the richest part of Mexico.

CHAPTER **6**

The Maya Today

In 1821, the Mexican people finally won their independence from Spain. The Yucatán became part of the new nation of Mexico, and the Maya were free people. But most had no way to support themselves except by working on haciendas. These haciendas were run as though they were towns, with their own laws, stores, chapels, and community events.

Mayans working on these estates were treated as slaves. The estate owners controlled them by making sure that they never got out of debt to the estate store—the only place the workers were allowed to buy food and other things they needed. As long as they owed money to the owner, they had to keep working for him.

The Yucatán chose to stay part of Mexico, although the local leaders often disagreed with the Mexican leaders. At the same time, the people of Guatemala, who were largely of Mayan descent, threw off Spanish rule and joined the new independent Mexico. (Two years later, Guatemala declared itself part of a separate country, the United Provinces of Central America.)

During the 1840s, there were several revolutions in Mexico. The government drafted Mayan men to fight the rebels, promising them land and lower taxes in return. But the government's promises were never kept. In 1847, angry Mayans started a rebellion called the Caste War. They bought weapons from the British government in neighboring Honduras. Led by educated Indian leaders, the Maya demanded fairer treatment. They said the government must give back peasant lands, apply the same laws to everyone, get rid of the debt system that enslaved them, and forbid the charging of fees for church sacraments.

The war was violent, with cruel acts on both sides. In March 1848, the Mayan rebels seemed on the brink of victory. But they stopped when they reached Mérida and did not invade the city. The rainy season had come, and many soldiers felt they must return home for the planting season. This

A young Guatemalan youth in a Quiché bell tower with a 50-caliber machine gun.

was part of their duty to their families and their religion. One soldier said, "if we do not (plant corn) we shall have no Grace of God (corn) to fill the bellies of our children."

The war raged on through 1849, however. By then, about half of the people in the Yucatán had died. Because there were fewer workers, the supply of corn and other foods dropped. The soldiers were hungry, sickly, and tired of fighting. Then a new religious movement called the Speaking Cross inspired them to keep on with their cause. But the rebels did eventually stop fighting, and the war ended in 1901. It was the most successful Indian rebellion ever fought in North America.

Meanwhile, modern times were coming to the Yucatán. By 1876, the industrial age had reached the region. The henequen industry made many landowners wealthy. In the United States, the invention of the reaper-binder had greatly increased grain crops. Bundles of grain had to be tied up, and the cheap twine made from henequen was in demand. Profits from this crop, called green gold, made the Yucatán the richest part of Mexico. Yet most Indians remained poor.

When the Caste War ended, the Mexican military occupied Chan Santa Cruz, a Mayan shrine city. In 1915, however, the government suddenly gave it back to the Maya. The

A Mayan child's drawing of an army helicopter firing bullets as people pray in front of a church.

Maya founded small villages in the area, based on the Speaking Cross religious cult. The Speaking Cross religion gave the Maya a link between their ancient beliefs and modern ways.

Other social changes were taking place in Mexico as a result of the revolution of 1910. People of Spanish descent no longer had more legal rights than the Indians of Meso-america. The Maya were able to get better educations and jobs. By 1924, the Mexican government was helping the Maya to start *ejidos* (farming villages) for themselves. Government land grants gave the Mayans a way to own property and earn more money and thus be more independent.

In the early 1930s, world henequen prices fell, and the Yucatán suffered a vast drop in income. It became one of Mexico's poorest areas. Besides a shortage of jobs, the area today has problems with crime, overpopulation, and political conflicts. The people did benefit from the improvement of schools, health care, and sanitation that began in the mid-1900s. The Yucatán has tried to boost its tourist industry and to find new products it can grow and make for export.

The Maya of Guatemala have experienced even worse hardships. About half of all Guatemalans (9.1 million) are Mayan. Most live in rural areas. Unlike Mexico, this country has not changed its social order since the days of the Spanish conquest. In Guatemala the Indians are still looked upon as inferior to people of Hispanic descent. They have lost their land and work for poor wages. For centuries, they have been overpowered by others—Spanish landowners, church officials, coffee plantation owners, and recently, by the military government. Powerful people have pushed Mayan farmers out of places with good soil and onto mountain slopes where farming is very difficult.

For a short period of time, between 1945 and 1954, the Guatemalan government set out to divide the land more fairly. President Jacobo Arbenz Guzman planned to give land to workers and start other social improvements.

The U.S. government strongly protested these changes. The American United Fruit Company (UFCO) was then the largest landowner in Guatemala. The company's officials thought they would lose its large income and tax-free benefits from its banana trade if the farmers got their own land. At the company's request, the U.S. State Department prevented the land grants.

The U.S. Central Intelligence Agency (CIA) and a branch of the U.S. Marine Corps helped a military colonel, Carlos Castillo, to overthrow the Guatemalan government. Violent fighting broke out. The new military government held unfair elections. Many of its officials were dishonest. Thousands of Guatemalan people fled from their country during these frightening years.

In later years, the economy of Guatemala got better through trade in coffee, cotton, and sugar. But only the wealthy got the benefits; the workers, mostly Indians, got poorer. About 300,000 Mayans traveled to coastal plantations each year, seeking jobs. They got very low wages for their labor. Many of these workers soon owed the plantation owners money for food and rent.

A woman named Cristina wrote about her family's misery as they harvested cotton and coffee on a Guatemalan plantation. She said, "The first child in my family to be killed died there because of the poison sprayed on the plants. After my brother died, my mother, who was packing coffee, kept him on her back the whole day. She waited until she had weighed the coffee before she put him down, and we buried him in a hole we dug behind

A Mayan festival in San Juan Chamula, located in Chiapas, Mexico. San Juan Chamula has become an important center of Mayan customs and religion.

the shelter where we slept with the rest of the workers. . . . None of them reported my brother's death because the boss would have fired all of us on the next day."

The Guatemalan government continues to use harsh methods to silence any protesters. People who call for social change or who are suspected of leading any uprisings are imprisoned or killed. Others have disappeared from their jobs, their homes, and the streets, and have not been seen since. The bodies of teachers, students, labor leaders, priests, and others are found in ditches, fields, and city dumps every day.

Some people have joined groups of guerrillas—rebels who live in hiding, often in the mountains. As the civil war in Guatemala has gone on, the government has forced men between the ages of 15 and 21 to join the army. Often, men escape from military service by joining the guerrillas. The army also forces men to join civilian patrol units. Armed with sticks, the patrols are expected to fight off the guerrillas, who carry guns. Sometimes, the guerrillas invade villages and threaten to hurt people unless they give them food, clothing, and other things.

More than 150,000 people have managed to escape Guatemala. These political refugees flee to Mexico and the United States.

In 1978, Andrés Avelino Zapeta y Zapeta, a brave farmer and carpenter, was elected mayor of Quiché, the ancient Mayan capital. Zapeta was the first Indian leader there in more than 200 years. He was admired for his hard work and devotion to his family, church, and community. In 1980, while he was walking to his field to hoe corn, Zapeta was murdered. The killing of this beloved political leader was heartbreaking to his followers.

In other cases, whole villages of Mayans have been murdered by soldiers. A priest named Ricardo Falla later described how 352 people were killed in Huehuetenango in 1982:

> At about 1:00 P.M. the soldiers began to fire at the women inside the small church. (Most were) taken to their homes in groups, and killed, the majority apparently with machetes (long knives). . . . Then they returned to kill the children, whom they had left crying and screaming by themselves. Then they continued with the men.

To get more protection, groups of villages have joined together in larger settlements.

A *Mayan woman grinding corn with a mano (handstone) and a metate (grinding slab).*

One such group of Chamula Mayans lives near the border of Guatemala. They are skilled farmers who have gotten jobs in their new community. Children can attend the local schools, and people have health care services. About 1 million Mayans from Guatemala now live in a Mexican Mayan region called Chiapas.

The two Mayan groups have blended parts of their cultures, although each has its own language, myths, and customs. Most of these people survive by raising corn on small fields and earning wages as day workers. They get jobs on coffee plantations and in the city of San Cristóbal.

The Maya of the Chamula region of Chiapas, Mexico, still suffer from the loss of their land during the 1500s. They have long fought to limit the destruction of forests there by the logging industry. San Juan Chamula has become an important center of Mayan customs and religion. The Mexican government helps the Maya to keep foreign influences out of the center.

People of Spanish descent are not allowed to live or own land in San Juan Chamula. Anyone who stays there overnight must get special permission. Important events and festivals are held at the Ceremonial Center and at the San Juan church. Each year, there is a large five-day celebration called Crazy

February. It requires weeks of preparation. The altars and shrines are covered with flowers. Special foods, including corn gruel and bean tamales, are made. The marketplace and churchyard are swept clean. The games and parades that follow have a religious meaning. The important Festival of Games, part of the Crazy February celebration, reminds people of events in Mayan history.

At the festivals, Mayan women show their creativity and religious devotion through their weavings. Many people admire the unique arts and crafts of the Maya. The pictures and symbols woven on *huipiles*—Mayan blouses—have special meanings. Patterns show the path of the sun and the moon and the stars. The Maya believe that huipil designs can be inspired by saints appearing in women's dreams.

The designs on cloth and clothing connect the Maya to their ancient past. They also show which community a person comes

Two women wearing huipiles *(Mayan blouses). The* huipil *designs have special meanings, inspired by saints appearing in dreams.*

from and where he or she lives. Today, many men wear store-bought shirts, then put traditional tunics over them. Besides weaving their families' clothing, women may weave cloth goods to sell. Or they may buy cloth and embroider fancy designs on it. A Mayan woman said that this weaving "shows people on the outside that we want to live, we don't want to die. I don't want to stop participating in my culture."

Today there are more than 10 million Mayans. Most look much like their ancestors: short and muscular, with broad heads, black hair, and dark skin. In rural families, men grow corn in their milpas. Today, there are digging sticks with metal tips, and a farmer can listen to music on a transistor radio as he works. Mayans still show a respect for nature, for corn, and for the rain. The women weave, cook, and take care of the children. In cities like Mérida, Guatemala City, and Mexico City, people work at different jobs, including those in industry and technology. They run computers and other machines.

Like people everywhere, Mayans want access to good education, decent health care, and equal legal rights. At the same time, they expect to be able to follow the ancient traditions and their own religion, if they choose. The Maya have worked long and hard to survive. Today, especially in Guatemala, they continue their courageous struggle. ▲

CHRONOLOGY

1500–100 B.C.	The Olmecs occupy what is today Veracruz, Mexico
1000 B.C.–A.D. 200	The trade center Kaminaljuyú flourishes
A.D. 100–700	Teotihuacán arises as the most important trading city in Central America
200–800	The Classic period, the earliest Mayan culture, develops in the northern part of the Yucatán Peninsula, with Tikal, Yaxchilan, Palenque, and Copán as the major centers of Classic Mayan life
ca. 800–1100	The Mayan culture blends with the Toltec-Mexican, resulting in changes in art, government, and religion
ca. 1200	The Toltec-Maya lose power; Mayapan replaces Chichén Itzá as the Yucatán capital
ca. 1400–1500	Feathered Serpent founds a new capital, Utatlán, and over-throws other leaders; Mesoamerica is now made up of several different states
1520	Spanish soldiers under Hernán Cortés conquer the Maya in Guatemala
1531–41	Spaniard Montejo the Younger divides the Mayan towns among his soldiers; some provinces in the West welcome the Spaniards, while the Mayans in the East resist
1546–1821	Mayans adopt some elements of Spanish and Mexican culture, including Catholicism; begin cultivating henequen and sugar-cane; increasing intermarriage between Mayans, Spanish, and Mexicans
1821	The Mexican people win independence from Spain, and the Yucatán becomes part of the new nation of Mexico
1847–1901	Mayans rebel against the Mexican government in the Caste War
ca. 1970–90	Civil war in Guatemala results in the death or exile of over 150,000 people

GLOSSARY

archaeologist a scientist who studies the remains of the life and culture of a people

chacmool a statue of a human figure lying on its back; its hands hold containers used for offerings

Classic period the earliest Mayan culture, which lasted from A.D. 250–900; the Mayans made great advances in mathematics, astronomy, and art during this time

Dresden Codex a manuscript from the Mayan's Post-classic period; a book of predictions, ceremonies, and movements of the stars and planets compiled by Mayan priests

ejidos farming villages that the Mexican government created for the Maya in 1924

hacienda a large plot of land owned by Spaniards, where Mayans worked and were treated like slaves

hieroglyphics written symbols representing an idea, an object, a syllable, or a sound

Mesoamerica middle or central America; the Mayans occupied this region, which includes the Yucatán Peninsula and part of Central America

Olmec a people who lived around the year 1500 B.C. in what is today Veracruz, Mexico; their lifestyle influenced the Mayans

Popul Vuh a sacred Mayan book; contains the creation legend and stories about Mayan history

quetzal a rare bird of Central America cherished by the Mayans because of its bright green feathers; the national bird of Guatemala

Toltec a people from the valley of Mexico who greatly influenced the Maya

INDEX

ABOUT THE AUTHOR

VICTORIA SHERROW holds B.S. and M.S. degrees from Ohio State University. The author of numerous stories and articles, she has also written 4 picture books and more than 20 works of nonfiction for children, including *Phillis Wheatley* in Chelsea House's JUNIOR WORLD BIOGRAPHY series, and *The Iroquois Indians* and *The Aztec Indians* in the JUNIOR LIBRARY OF AMERICAN INDIANS series. Sherrow lives in Connecticut with her husband, Peter Karoczkai, and their three children.

PICTURE CREDITS